# BLOOM

## Growing Money, People and Ministry

Jay Stearley, M.B.A., M.A.

Cover photo courtesy: Vladislav Reshetnyk
Headshot photos: Nick Torontali Photography

ESV Study Bible, English Standard Version. Wheaton: Crossway Bibles, 2007.
The Holy Bible, New International Version. Grand Rapids: Zondervan House, 1984.
Holy Bible: New American Standard Bible. Grand Rapids: Zondervan, 1995.
The Holy Bible: King James Version. Dallas: Brown Books Publishing, 2004.

Dedicated to those seeking first the Kingdom of God.

# Table of Contents

Prologue                                          9


SECTION I

Chapter 1: Foundations                           13

Chapter 2: Next-Level Moves for Churches         23

Chapter 3: Speak Up                              49

Chapter 4: Keep It Simple                        65

Chapter 5: Doing Business with God               73


SECTION II

Chapter 6: Leadership Workbook                   95


SECTION III

Appendix 1: Example Roadmap                      119

Appendix 2: Playbook                             125

Appendix 3: 52 Statistics                              135

Appendix 4: Ten Giving Reports to Utilize             141

Appendix 5: Money Talk Workshop                       143

Appendix 6: 131 Bible Verses on Resources            148

Appendix 7: Leader Impact Review                      156

Appendix 8: Ten Articles to Recommend                 157

Appendix 9: Growing Disciples Charts                  159

Appendix 10:Discipleship Roadmap                      160

Appendix 11: Deeper Discipleship Curriculum          161

Appendix 12: Give Yourself a $3,360 Raise            164

Appendix 13: Bloom Sermon Series                      167

About the Author                                      175

# Prologue

Generosity is a popular word and tactic used today by secular rappers and Christian preachers, businesses and nonprofits. Generosity comes with many positives, and it should certainly be celebrated. Yet, generosity is but one expression of a larger topic: stewardship.

Stewardship is the practice of taking care of resources. Resources can be hoarded or shared, increased or squandered, used for Jesus-worship or used for evil. When sagacious stewardship is employed, generosity can be multiplied; people and organizations move forward with peace and positive gospel impact.

It is therefore our responsibility as ministers to be educated, intentional, and discerning in regards to stewardship—leading a church, an organization, and ourselves to help others and impart the good news of Jesus. We must disciple people from a pure heart and the word of God to grow into spiritual maturity. We must raise the stewardship quotient in our own lives and the people we serve.

My aim is to help people mature spiritually, to equip leaders, and to fuel Kingdom work—blooming "like a tree planted by streams of water, which yields its fruit in season
and whose leaf does not wither—whatever they do prospers" (Psalm 1:3, NIV). Coaching and staffing are my vocation and calling, and I welcome the opportunity to be a trusted partner.

I am thankful to my wife and daughter, people who reviewed this material, and my teachers along the way. I am also thankful to K.P. Yohannan, Randy Alcorn, and James Milstead. Meeting you three and learning from your works and faith have been influential upon my life.

I pray that this book boosts your ministry resourcing through discipleship. Additional resources on a variety of topics are available at UpwardsForward.com.

# SECTION I

# Chapter 1

## Foundations

"The important thing is that you've got a strong
foundation before you start to try to save the world or
help other people."

Richard Branson

# Foundations

In 2017, Taewoong, a South Korean steel producer successfully casted a world record 1,000 millimeter round bloom.[12] Because of its high tensile strength and low cost, it (steel) is a major component used in buildings, infrastructure, tools, ships, trains, automobiles, machines, appliances, and weapons.[3]

Many of us will not set world records yet we all have areas of life and ministry that we would like to see bloom—to grow.

Resources will be needed to accomplish these things; to live and to expand gospel impact. Two components that contribute to the availability of resources are God's provision and stewardship. God's provision is the reality that God gives what He wills to people and organizations. Stewardship is how one looks after what God provides.

Many kinds of resources and/or assets are accessible. In the movie *Cast Away* (2000), the main

---

[1] www.sms-group.cn/english/press/press_release/376.html
[2] 3.2 feet
[3] https://en.wikipedia.org/wiki/Steel

character (played by Tom Hanks) was stranded on an island with "Wilson," his volleyball-turned-companion, and it was obvious how resources such as water, food, and shelter were paramount. Well, except for "Wilson." Organizations need additional resources, such as gathering spaces, people, computers, and cash. These resources can be real or financial assets. Real assets are income-generating assets such as land or equipment, whereas financial assets define the allocation of income or wealth among investors such as stocks or bonds.[4]

I need to define several terms prior to moving forward: resource, finance, capital, stewardship, and generosity.[5] People often use these terms interchangeably, yet they are unique.

- Resource: a stock or supply of money, materials, people, and other assets that can be drawn on by a person or organization in order to function effectively.

[4] Bodie, Kane, Marcus. *Investments, Fourth Edition.* Irwin/McGraw Hill, Boston, 1999, page 3.
[5] Definitions from Dictonary.com (2018)

- Finance: the management of large amounts of money, especially by governments or large companies.
- Capital: wealth in the form of money or other assets owned by a person or organization that is available or contributed for a particular purpose such as starting a company or investing.
- Stewardship: the job of supervising or taking care of something, such as an organization or property.
- Generosity: the quality of being sacrificial and/or extravagant.

As it pertains to God and the focus of this book, all resources are critical for the purpose of the Kingdom—the good news of Jesus and His will. And, when a person is biblically healthy in heart, soul, mind, and strength, their Kingdom impact is exponential. When an organization manages these matters wisely, its Kingdom impact is exponential—not just singularly to numbers and size, but additionally to quality and obedience.

God is very clear when it comes to the subject matter of this book. He doesn't simply prefer—He commands—that His people glorify Him with the resources He provides; we should be excellent stewards; we should be examples for the world to take notice.

According to Randy Alcorn of Eternal Perspective Ministries, "Stewardship is not a once-a-year consideration, but a week-to-week, month-to-month commitment requiring discipline and consistency."

The following is a sample of over hundreds of scriptures related to resources in the Bible[6]:

"For where your treasure is, there your heart will be also."
(Matthew 6:21, ESV)

"Whoever loves money never has enough; whoever loves wealth is never satisfied with their income."
(Ecclesiastes 5:10, NIV)

---

[6] See Appendix 5 for 131 Bible verses

"Know well the condition of your flocks and pay attention to your herds; For riches are not forever, nor does a crown endure to all generations."
(Proverbs 27:23-24, NASB)

"Make sure that your character is free from the love of money, being content with what you have; for He Himself has said, "I will never desert you, nor will I ever forsake you,"
(Hebrews 13:5, NASB)

"And all the tithe of the land, whether of the seed of the land, or of the fruit of the tree, is the Lord's: it is holy unto the Lord."
(Leviticus 27:30, KJV)

"Instruct them to do good, to be rich in good works, to be generous and ready to share,"
(1 Timothy 6:18, NASB)

"You shall generously give to Him, and your heart shall not be grieved when you give to Him, because

for this thing the Lord your God will bless you in all your work and in all your undertakings."
(Deuteronomy 15:10, NASB)

"Look! The wages you failed to pay the workers who mowed your fields are crying out against you. The cries of the harvesters have reached the ears of the Lord Almighty."
(James 5:4, NIV)

No matter your life or ministry focus, resources matter. Each of us must be aware and wise about them. Focusing energy and intentionality towards them will yield significant improvements in all things . . . and danger.

Beware. Nobody is above or beyond temptation towards monetary or status gain.

"For the love of money is a root of all sorts of evil, and some by longing for it have wandered away from the faith and pierced themselves with many griefs."
(1 Timothy 6:10, NASB)

"Nor thieves nor the greedy nor drunkards nor slanderers nor swindlers will inherit the kingdom of God."

(1 Corinthians 6:10, NIV)

"Put to death, therefore, whatever belongs to your earthly nature: sexual immorality, impurity, lust, evil desires and greed, which is idolatry."

(Colossians 3:5, NIV)

Worship is also an important element of stewardship. It is the act of giving back to God and investing in the Kingdom of God. All that God entrusts to an individual or organization should be utilized in a spirit of worship—ascribing worth, reverence, surrender, and devotion.

# Application Questions

## Chapter 1: Foundations

1. What resources has God placed in your charge?

2. What could your resources become with improved stewardship?

3. How could the Kingdom of God benefit from your resources?

4. Where does greed creep into your life?

5. What Bible verse from this chapter affected you and why?

6. How can you use precision praise (specific and meaningful) to encourage others in these matters?

# Action Items

## Chapter 1: Foundations

1.  Fast and pray over your, and your organization's, stewardship.

2.  Discuss and align philosophy and issues related to resourcing.

3.  Take inventory of your resources.

4.  Acquire professional counsel to gain clarity on resource reality.

5.  Develop a strategic plan with processes for stewardship.

6.  Attain tools to account for resources.

# Chapter 2

## Next-Level Moves for Churches

"Progress is impossible without change, and
those who cannot change their minds
cannot change anything."

George Bernard Shaw

# Next-Level Moves for Churches

Personal resource stewardship bleeds into organizational stewardship and generosity, where I focus now: leading ministry.

One church was growing at a quick clip. She was labeled by *Outreach Magazine* as being one of North America's fastest growing churches in America (2016). Many factors contributed to this reality, including God's grace, wonderful people, and intentionality. Two specific key factors in this church's success were developing a culture of generosity and operating according to a strategic plan, including the budget. But, these things did not happen overnight. They took time and consistent determination (i.e., prayer, focus, willpower, purpose). It took that church nearly four years to break through next-level barriers.

Prior to making changes for growth, I remember asking this church's lead pastor, "How did you get here?" He replied without hesitation, "God's grace."

I remember thinking, "That is beautiful faith!" and "Just think what is possible if we employ intentionality to all areas of the ministry!".

Churches face six common areas for growth: strategy, budgeting, staffing, compensation, generosity initiatives, and discipleship.

## Strategy

Many people love Jesus. Many people lead gospel-centered ministries. Few know how to get where they've been called.

Strategic planning helps. It is the process of intentional focus by leadership to gain clarity on reality, define action steps, and employ accountability rhythms. The Paterson Center StratOp is an excellent process to attain this; I am a certified StratOp facilitator.

Strategy comes naturally to some. It is a marker of Gallup's CliftonStrengths[7] assessment. Every ministry team benefits from having this type of person on their team, whether an insider or adjunct partner. Strategists help orchestrate how to get where the calling is and how to attain the vision.

A good friend of mine is wired for strategy. I call him "King Midas" because it seems that everything he touches turns into gold. (He hates it when I call him this.)

---

[7] Tom Rath. *Strengths Finder*. New York, 2017.

He fears God. Yet, the reality exists that he is successful with the plans and moves he makes. He is very strategic, consults wise counselors, and takes the time to develop and initiate plans.

For strategic planning, using the right tools is also essential. Tools provide the necessary information to see reality clearly and then to make the appropriate moves. Two of these important tools are a robust Church Management System (ChMS) and a monetary trends application.

Once a strategic plan is developed, one option to use is the approach of *The Four Disciplines of Execution*[8] for follow-through. These are (1) focusing on the wildly important, (2) acting on lead measures, (3) keeping a compelling scoreboard, and (4) creating a cadence of accountability.

Strategic planning is accountable leadership unto God with what He has entrusted us: stewardship.

---

[8] McChesney, Covey, Huling. *The Four Disciplines of Execution*. New York, Franklin Covey, 2012.

## Budgeting

As an executive pastor, I cut 8 percent out of the church budget within the first year; hundreds of thousands of dollars of fluff—unused satellite television, copier contracts, untimely consulting agreements, and more. As a leadership team, we looked in the mirror and asked ourselves, "Where do we need to invest resources, not simply pay the bills?" This was a significant paradigm shift away from, "How do we manage?"

Another mistake we were making was cutting costs equally across the board each year to make the budget work. What we lost during those few years of stewardship was precious Kingdom time and accelerated ministry progress. We came to understand that strategic initiatives should take precedent. In other words, we needed to keep "the main thing the main thing." No longer would we cut expenses across the board. No, we would allocate the necessary resources towards strategic initiatives first, and do our best with the remainder of the ministry.

According to Malphurs and Stoope, "A strategic budget guides the church in allotting and spending its money in congruence with its deep, defining core values to accomplish a specific, biblical mission a clear, compelling vision. It follows the basics of a good budget but focuses on where God is taking the church."[9]

Two words of caution. First, don't be a cheapskate. Rather, be intentionally wise, missional, and generous. Second, remain flexible; follow the Spirit, take strategic steps, and receive returns on investment.

You may have heard the phrase, "It takes money to make money." This means that it takes an outlay of resources to attain gain. You can apply this to discipleship, gardening, weightlifting, etc. In order to experience a resource revival, ministries must begin to steward resources with strategic intentionally that takes into account investment—bang for your buck. Investing is resourcing what matters most to yield the desired return.

## Staffing

People are the primary difference makers. They alone take you to new heights! Buildings are nice, but without people, they sit empty. Books are pretty, but

---

[9] Malphurs, Stoope. *Money Matters in Church.* Baker Books, Grand Rapids. 2007. Page 53.

without someone to read them, they're worthless. Knowledge is nice, but without action, it too is worthless.

Having the right people in the right places with the right clarity of expectations matters—this is alignment. Calling, personality, experience, and spiritual giftings contribute to the perfect fit. Oftentimes, people are simply in the wrong places. Other times, they are the wrong person altogether (this is harder than the former). Talent and the organization matter.

Ministries must not only discern what jobs need to be done, but also what it will take to increase growth. For example, one available pastor on staff for a site of over 3,000 adults could be a relational growth barrier. If it is crucial to serve children and their caretakers, yet a church "can't" afford staffing that ministry appropriately, perhaps it is time to restructure staff or stop doing some other ministry. Another often overlooked and undervalued element to increased growth, is retaining amazing people on our teams. Monty Kelso, President of Slingshot Group, gives us the main ingredient to keeping next-level people:

Ultimately, people don't leave a job because of compensation, frustration over the role, or the city they live in. More consistently than any other factor they leave because they don't feel that they are fully valued

Keep good people for the long-haul by not treating them like a tool or a talent, but rather a treasure. Take time out of your day, find margin in your life and in your work, where you can invest in the lives of your staff so that they feel as though they are a treasure.[10]

People also need adequate tools and training to fulfill their callings and job. This may be a new curriculum, a computer program, an expense account to take key leaders out for a coffee, or a technology. Doing so will help develop a generous culture, an effective ministry, and an influx of resources like time, treasure, and talents.

## Compensation

Anthony the Great was an ascetic. He denied himself all pleasures of life and the common culture way of life. He lived years at a time atop a wooden platform in the

---

[10] Slingshot Group. *Valuing People with Monty Kelso.* YouTube, 2019.

desert. He gave up the compensation and the esteem of the world to pursue Christ. Most people then, and now, do not choose nor receive this calling, yet we must pause to appreciate the sacrifice and devotion.

The opposite of an ascetic is a sybaritic, one who is characterized by or loving luxury or sensuous pleasure.[11] One could describe King Solomon, for a season, as a sybaritic.[12] Yet, he learned that this lifestyle was errant and not satisfying. Lauren Greenfield's documentary, "Generation Wealth," is a riveting modern look a this lifestyle.[13]

As stewards and overseers of workers, we need to disciple people in the ways of biblical stewardship, and to take care of people well—to not "muzzle the ox."[14] This matters not only to the individual but to their families and friends as well. To ask for sacrifice is biblical, yet not to the extent of demanding asceticism. Likewise, to bless people lavishly is biblical, yet not to the extent of hedonism nor sybaritic-inducing.

---

[11] Dictionary.com, 2019
[12] Ecclesiastes 2:1-11
[13] Greenfield, L. (Director). (2018) *Generation Wealth* [Motion Picture]. United States: Amazon.
[14] I Corinthians 9:9; I Timothy 5:18

Slingshot Group partnered with David Fletcher of XPastor.org in 2018 on a series of workshops for Executive and Operational Pastors named "Smart Money." David said this about compensation:

> The starting pay for staff is likely the most important decision to make—and maybe the hardest.

> If starting pay is too low and that is realized too late, giving such a large raise later may be hard for the congregation to understand. Starting too low might mean the staff member settles for a smaller house or a less desirable neighborhood; raising their salary to a fair level is unlikely to compensate them for the cost or annoyance of moving.

> If starting pay is too high and the staff member excels, giving a raise and bonus may not be affordable for the church. Also it could result in unjustifiable compensation compared to other paid positions in the church.

Base pay salary is also just the beginning. Other benefits such as health insurance for the employee and family (if applicable), paid time off, continuing education, housing incentives (i.e., down payment on a home), and even bonuses are important to consider. According to Weese and Crabtree, "A good retention plan not only helps avoid unnecessary and costly leadership transitions, but is a good selling point in recruiting a new pastor."[15]

Compensating people for their work is essential, and God commands it (James 5:4). Yet, often leaders speak of sacrifice. "If you were committed to the mission, you'd take less money." Wrong!

You can see a person's commitment to the mission apart from money with things such as time, loyalty, and more. This isn't to say they shouldn't be giving generously to the immediate ministry, but there is a larger picture.

Do what you can to compensate, appreciate, and honor workers in your ministry. Do your research. Justifiable investment in people will undeniably yield long-term savings and high job satisfaction—guaranteed!

---

[15] Weese, Crabtree. *The Elephant in the Boardroom.* Jossey-Bass, San Francisco, 2004, page 80.

People need to be properly compensated, resourced, appreciated, and aligned. Doing ministry staffing as a vocation, I see churches lose and/or also fail to recruit top-tier staff over amounts as small at $2,000. This is a mistake. It costs exponentially more than this amount to manage change, recruit, replace, retrain, and regain momentum—let alone the relational and emotional impacts to the organization.

People need to be appreciated. O.C. Tanner is a company that helps over 13.5 million people accomplish and appreciate great work. Their research shows that 79 percent of employees who quit their jobs claim that a lack of appreciation was a major reason for leaving. You can appreciate people in  many ways, and different people value different kinds of appreciation. For example, many people love public recognition, but others shy away from it. Some love a simple movie gift card, and others prefer a note. The point is, know your people and appreciate them in the best ways possible, and often.

## Generosity Initiatives

Stewardship is essential, yet without a culture of generosity, effectiveness will always be tempered.

Organizations will not reach their full potential, nor will people grow to spiritual maturity without proper stewardship. Additionally, people decreasingly attend church in person, so it is necessary to provide ways to give, such as online or via mobile devices available every day of the week.

Generosity initiatives are far more than compensation or a budget: they involve calculated communications, discipleship, and stewardship. Popular initiatives in churches today include capital campaigns or offering Dave Ramsey's *Financial Peace University*. These alone, however, rarely breed a culture of generosity for the masses long-term. Organizations need to be consistent with stewardship efforts throughout the entire organization, to model it all the time, and to stay up to date.

Before providing examples of how to boost a culture of generosity, consider the following statistics (see Appendix 2 for additional statistics):

- Giving to religion is estimated to have declined by 1.5% in 2018 (a decrease of 3.9% adjusted for inflation). (Giving USA, 2019)

- U.S. Americans gave about 3% of their disposable income to churches in 1968, and less than 2.2% in 2016. (Empty Tomb, 2016)

- Credit card balances carried from one month to the next hit $443.96 billion in September 2019, according to NerdWallet's annual analysis of U.S. household debt. Credit card debt has increased almost 6% in the past year and more than 34% in the past five years. (Nerdwallet, 2019)

- 37% of regular church attendees and Evangelicals don't give money to church. (Nonprofits Source, 2018)

- Nearly 7 in 10 American adults (69 percent) making $60,000 or more of household income say they donated money over the last year, compared with less than half of people (45 percent) in households making less than $40,000. (Barna, 2013)

- Total giving to charitable organizations was $410.02 billion in 2017 (2.1 percent of GDP). This is an increase of 5.2 percent in current dollars and 3 percent in inflation-adjusted dollars from 2016. (Giving USA, 2018)

- About 1 in 5 American (U.S.) families who make $41,200 or less have what's considered a hefty debt burden—defined as more than 40 percent debt-to-income load. (CNN Wires, 2015)

- 49 percent of all church giving transactions are made with a card. (Nonprofits Source, 2018)

- 49 percent of baby boomer donors are enrolled in a monthly giving program. (Nonprofits Source, 2018)

The following are ten examples of how to boost a culture of generosity:

1. Pray

2. Utilize discipleship metrics to target discipleship (i.e., new guests, the baptized, small group participation, leaders)

3. Utilize financial giving data to target discipleship (i.e., new givers, lapsed givers, giving groups)

4. Pursue and disciple monetary givers

5. Make giving easy taking into account age demographic preferences, trends, and starting-points (i.e. text to give, crowdfunding, differing amounts)

6. Lavish your staff and leaders often

7. Produce regular vision-heavy communication pieces

8. Build into all of your discipleship efforts talking points on stewardship

9. Provide compelling opportunities to give, especially during October through December (30 percent of annual giving to nonprofits happens in December; Nonprofits Source, 2018)

10. Regularly invest in the needs of your neighborhood, city, and the globe; model and celebrate often

Each of these examples makes a positive difference. One in particular has a high yield: pursue and disciple monetary givers. In addition to cultivating a culture of generosity, the aim of this initiative is to value, love, connect, and partner with people for gospel impact. Here's how it all works:

1.  Pray

2.  Fast

3.  Identify people who give or have given

4.  Divide these people into groups according to giving markers (i.e., new givers, lapsed givers, long-term givers)

5.  Select, train, and empower a team(s) to pursue givers (this is about far more than money or talking about money)

6.  Track results

A common question I receive is, "What does a conversation look like with a lapsed or a stopped giver?" Here are the elements to the call or visit:

1.  Greet and then identify who you are

2.  Communicate that you are calling to say hello, to be a help, and to pray for them

3. Ask simple questions about their life (i.e., family, hobbies, work)

4. Ask if there is anything you can help them with regarding the church (i.e., answer questions, help them connect)

5. Ask how you can pray for them

6. Pray with them right then

7. Bless and end

You will be amazed what a simple call like this does. You will learn about their lives—perhaps of health battles or opportunities to care for people. People will return to YHWH-God. People will grow spiritually. People will feel loved. You will gain new volunteers. You may even be attacked...and much more!

## Discipleship

Where I live, Nevada, United States, buffets are popular. They are perfect for tourists and locals alike, consuming whatever they desire. One even boasts of having eight live action stations, where you can order pho, charcuterie, or a salad just as you like, right before your eyes.

Oftentimes church discipleship strategies are like a buffet: all sorts of programs are offered, and then leaders hope for the best.

Another approach to discipleship is to be specifically targeted, intentional, and progressive. Keeping with the food parallel, one could call this amuse-bouche. This is when a chef selects a small, special hors-d'oeuvre to serve a guest, oftentimes showcasing what is to come. It is very intentional and and timely.

Amuse-bouche-like discipleship systems are powerful in helping people grow in the faith. They provide the proper connection points for every individual and ongoing pathways to mature. Intentional discipleship systems also build synergy throughout a ministry. They help people understand the next steps for growth, they help connect people, and they foster appreciation amongst ministry leaders and teamwork.

Buffets may be great for food, but not for discipleship; it depends on the consumer. Amuse-bouche is great for food, and for discipleship; it develops healthy disciples and grows congregations.

The following are discipleship truths to contemplate and to tailor make for your ministry.[16] These truths capture the progressive experience of people and the necessities to mature disciples. A few words of warning, don't let it paralyze you; don't delay implementation because you don't have everything figured out. I see too many churches with the heart and agreement to disciple, but never launch a lasting effort because they don't know all the details. This is tragic. People need spiritual food and will follow your lead—just get going! "Worship in the Spirit and the truth" and "love from a pure heart and a good conscience and a sincere faith."[17][18]

**Growth Wheel**: People grow spiritually when they encounter God, have community, and worship.

**Growth Curve**: People grow in maturity over time.

**Growth Team**: People with pastoral, administration, and production aptitudes.

---

[16] Appendix 9
[17] John 4:24
[18] I Timothy 1:5

**Growth Sequence**: People need discipleship experiences that increase in commitment, depth, and width over time.

**Programming Example**

1. Introductory

    a. Witnesses: champion and commission people to be active to share the good news everywhere and anywhere.

    b. Virtual: develop communications for people to interact online, and a system for reaching out to people via phone, cards, text, etc.

    c. Worship gatherings.

    d. Get-to-know-each-other gatherings (i.e., 5-minute meet and greet, 1.5-hour meal with relationship building, Q&A)

2. Transitional

    a. *Begin*: a four-week experience that helps people make friends, understand the gospel, and take steps forward in the faith.[19]

---

[19] *Begin*. Jay Stearley, 2017.

b. *Rooted*: a 10-week experience that is designed to deepen your connection with God, His Church, and your purpose and that is a catalyst for life change.[20]

c. Care ministries (i.e., Celebrate Recovery[21], DivorceCare[22])

3. Solidifying

    a. Life groups: four-month or longer small groups where the rhythms of relationship, mission, prayer, and study take place.

    b. Mission groups: opportunities for people to volunteer, serve others, travel, etc.

    c. Worship gatherings

4. Enduring

    a. Resources

---

[20] www.experiencerooted.com
[21] www.celebraterecovery.com
[22] www.divorcecare.org/

b. *Deeper*: a 12-month experiential scholarship in three categories of doctrine, missiology, and leadership.[23]

c. Worship gatherings

d. Retreats

e. Workshops

Another important aspect of discipleship is helping people discover and develop their spiritual gift(s).[24] This is done and confirmed through community, not a person's solo declaration. I like how Thomas Schreiner puts it, encouraging people to not simply use spiritual test questionnaires for discovery, "Spiritual gifts can't be traced in a laboratory like DNA."[25]

God bestows spiritual gifts on each of His children for the service, maturing, and building up of the church in various ways.[26][27] Specific to the topic stewardship is the spiritual gift of metadidomi or giver.[28] Dr. Gilbert, author of  defines this gift as "(having) the Spirit-given capacity

---

[23] Appendix 11

[24] Romans 12; I Corinthians 12; Ephesians 4; 1 Peter 4

[25] Schreiner, Thomas. *Spiritual Gifts: What They Are and Why They Matter*. B&H Books, 2018.

[26] I Corinthians 7:7; 2 Timothy 1:6

[27] 1 Peter 4:10; Ephesian 4:12-13

[28] Romans 12:8

and desire to serve God by giving of your material resources, far beyond the tithe (10%), to further the work of God.[29] Many people give more than a tithe who may not have the spiritual gift of giving, yet the point is that some do have a supernatural disposition, ability, and practice of generosity.

The church needs giver-gifted people just as teachers and servants are needed. It is therefore a responsibility of church ministers and overseers to encourage, equip, and employ this gifting for the good of the body and the Kingdom of God.

---

[29] Gilbert, Larry. *Your Gifts: Discover God's Unique Design for You.* ChurchGrowth.org, 2015.

# Application Questions

## Chapter 2: Next-Level Moves for Churches

1. Where do you need to strategically update your organization's budget?

2. How are you creating a remarkable team?

3. How do you communicate about resources?

4. How do you offer opportunities for generosity growth and also model it?

5. How do you know when someone makes a change in their giving to the ministry?

6. Why is it biblical to disciple people in stewardship?

7. When will you have strategic planning meetings on boosting your generosity culture?

# Action Items

## Chapter 2: Next-Level Moves for Churches

1. Fast and pray over your, and your organization's, stewardship.

2. Participate in a professional strategic planning process such as StratOp.

3. Create a strategic budget that aligns to the strategic plan.[30]

4. Staff according to the strategic plan.

5. Foster a healthy culture.

6. Research market-based compensation and surpass in generosity.

7. Develop and employ a comprehensive generosity initiative.

---

[30] Malphurs, Stroope. *Money Matters in Church*. Baker Books, Grand Rapids. 2007, page 53.

# Chapter 3

## Speak Up

"Leave safety behind. Put your body on the line. Stand before the people you fear and speak your mind even if your voice shakes. When you least expect it, someone may actually listen to what you have to say. Well-aimed slingshots can topple giants."

Maggie Kuhn

# Speak Up

"I have a dream," proclaimed the late and great Martin Luther King, Jr. What was delivered to a live crowd of some 250,000 and a television audience of millions became a pinnacle moment for civil rights for all time. But, what if he never spoke up and heeded the call upon his life that ultimately lead to his death? Either a delay in biblical matters or nothing at all. Yet, he did, and so must we.

Sometimes it is difficult or awkward for us to speak about resources and money, whether with a spouse or a neighbor—let alone the church. However, Jesus nor the apostles ever hesitated to talk about this topic. People today talk about it regularly too[31]:

- 75 percent of people ages 18–34 talk about money weekly
- 66 percent of people ages 35–54 talk about money weekly

---

[31] "One Third of Consumers Live Paycheck to Paycheck." TD Bank, Jul 26, 2018.

- 44 percent of people ages 55+ talk about money weekly

Carey Nieuwhof, Pastor of Connexus Church, recommends these seven ways to "get past the funk": realize people talk about money every day; view talking about money as pastoral care; help people plan their financial future, not just yours; understand you're slaying a giant idol; tap into the desire to be generous; your vision and stewardship must be worth the sacrifice people make; unchurched people are more open to conversation about money than you realize.[32]

Money is a common idol and hindrance to peoples' faith. It is an indicator of the inner man. Yet, it is a necessary resource for our gospel efforts. It is therefore extremely important that we talk and teach about resources in ways that are not grating nor guilting.

Speaking about money also becomes easier when we have clarity on what we're called to and how we're going to get there. These give us a sense of passionate conviction and build trust with givers. Most people,

---

[32] https://careynieuwhof.com/7-ways-to-to-get-past-the-funk-of-talking-about-money-at-church/#comments

especially large givers, like to know where and how their money will be used. A track record of tangible results and donations demonstrates the organization's ability to perform in a spiritual manner.

Some reasons that people do not give are lack of biblical understanding and lack of trust, they aren't Jesus followers, they do not understand how funds are used, they see waste or misuse, they are not on board with the organization, they don't know giving is a part of their worship, giving fatigue, they are not moved by The Spirit nor vision, and they are not recognized or appreciated . . . the list goes on and on. No matter the reason, skirting around the topic of biblical stewardship is not an option. Leaders need to get over their trepidation and make the conversation about money and resources safe and healthy.

It is leadership's responsibility to train people to see their stewardship and giving as worship and investing in God's Kingdom. We must update our communications and programming to walk with people on their journey. They need to be purposeful, specific, easy to access, and timely.

## Imagine

Imagine a church where no capital campaigns were needed to fund its work. Additionally, imagine the global impact if every Jesus follower lived with obedience and generosity. *Relevant Magazine*[33] did that, looking at what North American Christians could accomplish if everyone gave at least 10 percent, equivalent to an additional $165 billion. Here is what they found:

- $25 billion could relieve global hunger, starvation, and deaths from preventable diseases in five years.

- $12 billion could eliminate illiteracy in five years.

- $15 billion could solve the world's water and sanitation issues, specifically at places in the world where 1 billion people live on less than $1 per day.

- $1 billion could fully fund all overseas mission work.

---

[33] "What Would Happen if the Church Tithed," Mike Holmes, March 8, 2016.

- $100–$110 billion would still be left over for additional ministry expansion.

Imagine the positive impact on marriages and families if money was not such a stressor, if they understood how to deal with resources, utilize a budget, prepare for the future, etc. Imagine the impact we can have in the workplace too.[34] [35]

- The number of employees saying that financial matters cause everyday stress is more than those who answered with any other life stressor combined.
- 65 percent of women and 52 percent of men said that financial matters cause them the most stress.
- 35 percent of employees report that issues with personal finances have been a distraction at work. Nearly half (49 percent) of those who are distracted by their finances at work say

---

[34]

www.pwc.com/us/en/private-company-services/publications/assets/pwc-2019-employee-wellness-survey.pdf

[35] www.moneyhabitudes.com/financial-statistics/

that they spend three hours or more at work
each week thinking about or dealing with
issues related to their personal finances.

- Employees admit that financial worries have
  impacted their health, relationships,
  productivity, and time away from work.

Loving, teaching, discipling, serving, and leading
people further is the answer. Speak up. Call people to
action. Cast vision. Share stories. Be comfortable. Model
generosity. Be obedient and intentional.

## Multiply

Speaking about resources from the stage only goes
so far. Offering an optional discipleship class goes even
shorter. It is therefore vital to speak up in all areas of
ministry. This requires equipping, empowering, and
sending others to speak up as well.

To carry out effective communication, we must
repeat the heart and vision, along with talking points, to
influencers (i.e., staff, leaders), beginning with the
leadership core and moving outwards—first to primary

decision-makers, to staff, to ministry teams, to leaders, then to the masses. Utilize unique gatherings as well in the distributing of information.

A team focused on resources is also needed—administrators and distributors. Someone will be needed to set up and track the monetary details, another will be needed to report and track contact lists, ful distributors are needed. I use the word *masterful* because these team members make or break initiatives. They need to be respected, astute, and relationally dynamic.

## Approach

Half Dome is a 1,362-foot cliff in Yosemite National Park, California, United States. A person can summit the dome via multiple routes. The most popular route is to hike to the "cables," which then aids the path of the last 400 feet of elevation to the summit. Others choose direct routes up the sheer face of the dome on rock climbs such as the Regular Northwest Face. No matter how you reach the summit, an approach is required.

I have summited Half Dome only twice, once using the "cables" and another time via the Snake Dike rock climb. On the latter, we descended on what is known as the

Death Slabs approach that services the sheer face. It is a sketchy proposition and challenge that left me exhausted, a bit frazzled, and scratched up.

When we size up our approach to speaking up about money and resources, we must know our summit and routes. This involves having a clear picture of the desired results, both for the individual and ministry, and also the channels for communication success.

Desired results will be unique to each ministry. For instance, some may seek freedom from debt or the ability to make gathering space improvements. When it comes to individuals, results will be unique too. In either case, the Bible outlines best practices for us to champion. They are freedom over debt, preparation for the future, and generosity.[36]

In order to attain these three summits, our approaches need to have consistent messaging through multiple channels that foster penetrating saturation. For example, one slide on Sunday with an invite to a finance webinar and an email from a general church mailbox will not penetrate to the audience on its own, especially if there are ten other rotating slides, plus verbal announcements,

---

[36] Proverbs 22:7; Proverbs 6:6–11; Proverbs 22:9.

weekly updates update emails, and more, all on other aspects of the ministry.

Messaging must be calculated and precise in today's environment of oversaturated communications and stimulus.[37]

## Shift

I spent a wet fall repairing part of the transmission on my motorcycle. The first dry day after the repairs, I took it for a ride. The gears shifted smoothly and quietly. The smile was wide on my face!

Smack! Eleven minutes later I was rear ended by a four-door sedan traveling at over 50 mph. I was severely broken and so was my freshly repaired bike.

I had to make a shift: no longer could I or would I ride on a public street again; no longer would my motorcycle make a shift. The good news for me was God's providence over my life, stewardship preparations previously made by me and my organization, and modern

---

[37]

www.theguardian.com/science/2015/jan/18/modern-world-bad-for-brain-daniel-j-levitin-organized-mind-information-overload medical care. I am back to living and riding. I carry scars and pain, yet the present future is bright.

The present future is also bright for our organizations. Never before have we had access to such easy and amazing tools. Never before has society shared so much information nor addressed stewardship. A shift has taken place.

Due to non-biblical stewardship, scandals, privacy, and abuse, people and ministries can be shy or afraid to speak about money and other resources. Some would even say, "We just trust God, and whatever happens will happen." This is the right kind of faith, but abhorrent stewardship.

The Lord instructs us to be biblical stewards and to instruct others towards maturity. This is non-negotiable to our spiritual callings. Therefore, we must speak up about money and resources.

In addition to our spiritual instruction, society at large is beginning to wrestle with and to speak about stewardship. This is due to a number of phenomena such as modern technologies, younger people entering the job force with different values than those before them, debt escape, and the popularity of generosity campaigns.

Let us then "shift gears" to make a gospel impact in people's lives through stewardship discipleship.

# Application Questions

## Chapter 3: Speak Up

1. What bullet point above challenges you the most and why?

2. How will you increase your communications about money, resources, and generosity?

3. What steps in your personal life do you need to take to achieve next level stewardship?

4. Who can you lean on for advice and coaching?

5. What coaching does your communications team need? (i.e., web, print, stage)

6. What hesitancies do you have in communicating about resources and why?

# Application Questions

## Chapter 3: Speak Up

1. Fast and pray over your, and your organization's, stewardship.

2. Define at least five results of what is possible with adequate resourcing.

3. Define at least ten talking points about stewardship.

4. Celebrate often with people and share stories about godly stewardship.

5. Appoint the appropriate person(s) to oversee and champion the strategic plan for resourcing.

6. Schedule resourcing-driven gatherings, communications, and discipleship measures.

7. Meet with ministry leaders to understand resourcing, their practice, and their influence.

8. Meet with select monetary givers.

9. Publish regular communication pieces that cast

vision and share ministry stories and results.

# Chapter 4

## Keep It Simple

"Simplicity is the key to brilliance."

Bruce Lee

# Keep It Simple

After a semester of teaching how to build weighted portfolios of investments in graduate school, my professor stood at the front of the room with the *Wall Street Journal* in his hand. He tacked it up to the wall, stepped back, and began throwing darts at it. He then made the following statement:

> You can do all the analyzation you want. But in the end, you never know what will happen. There is sometimes not much greater percentage gain in building portfolios, as there is in simply shooting darts at a paper and choosing the stocks the darts hit.

I withdrew from the finance department, stopped my internship at a global brokerage house, and switched to a specialization in management soon after.

Managing resources can be very difficult. Yes, advanced systems and tools are needed, but basic best practices always guide the way:

1.  Glorify God

2.  Ensure that people trump money

3.  Be resourceful

4.  Be diversified

5.  Don't spend more than you bring in

6.  Keep some of your assets liquid

7.  Have no debt or a low debt-to-income ratio

8.  Have solid checks and balances

9.  Work a calculated strategy

10. Know contentment and purposefulness

Remember the parable of the talents—invest and utilize[38]; keep the bulk of liquid assets in an inflation-tracking interest rate at a minimum, make investments for the Kingdom, and always be generous.

Today, many tools are available regarding resources for personal and organizational matters. They afford keen

---

[38] Matthew 25:14-30

insights and even reminders to stay on track. Research the tools that are right for you and that also have the ability to interact with other applications, and use them. And lest we forget, solid discipleship opportunities and resources are available such as "Money Talks" workshops[39], small group curriculums, and much more.

Chapter 2 and Section III of this book provide more in depth sample game plans and action steps for ministries. The gists of the way of stewardship are:

- Address the heart
- Gain clarity
- Create a plan
- Take action
- Be consistent

These five elements need to be reviewed and adjusted regularly.

## Change Management

No matter your organization's barriers, fostering an environment where updates and change can take place in a

---

[39] Appendix 5

healthy manner is important. The alternatives are church splits, church closings, or even damage to people's faith journeys.

*Leading Congregational Change*[40] outlines the following to foster change well: accurately assess and describe current reality, make information widely available, seek assistance, conduct a congregational assessment, and make honesty and constructive criticism the accepted and expected behavior. This last element is arguably the most important element.

VitalSmarts® interviewed 1,025 managers of organizations and found that of those who managed growing organizations, 100 percent exercised what they termed crucial conversations, which are discussions between two or more people with high stakes, varied opinions, and strong emotions. To successfully conduct these types of conversations, start with the heart, learn to look, make it safe, master your stories, STATE your path, explore others' paths, and move to action.[41]

---

[40] Herrington, Bonem, Furr. *Leading Congregational Change.* Jossey-Bass, San Francisco, 2000. Pages 37-40.
[41] Patterson, Grenny, McMillan, Switzler. *Crucial Conversations.* McGraw-Hill, 2012.

Change will happen. Our responsibility is to make it as clear and supportive as possible. Doing so will help people move past initial fear, doubt, and paralyzation. And, at the end of the day, if we have done everything in our ability to be upright and consistent with a gospel heart, the Lord will do His will and reward each person according to their deeds.[42]

There is urgency with gospel—it is time to be next-level stewards with the resources God entrusts to us!

---

[42] I Corinthian 4:1–5

# Application Questions

## Chapter 4: Keep It Simple

1. Which three practices out of the ten are your strongest?

2. Which three practices out of the ten are your weakest?

3. About what do you need to speak to your spouse or leadership team in regards to resources?

4. If I were in your shoes, what advice would you give to me?

5. How can you make your stewardship practices simpler and more effective?

6. When do you need to have a conversation about the budget?

# Action Items

## Chapter 4: Keep It Simple

1. Fast and pray over your, and your organization's, stewardship.

2. Make resourcing systems streamlined, synergistic, and applicable.

3. Build a remarkable team.

# Chapter 5

## Doing Business with God

"My mouth will speak words of wisdom; the meditation of
my heart will give you understanding."

Sons of Korah (Psalm 49:3)

# Doing Business with God

I wish I could tell you that I do not have a propensity towards greed. I like outdoor gear. I like security. I've been trained to build wealth. However, I need to do business with God frequently to align with His purposes for my life and those with whom I work. This involves meditating on God's Word, examining my heart, taking stock of my resources, seeking counsel, and praying.

Four Bible passages that I meditate on regularly are:

"But godliness with contentment is great gain. For we brought nothing into the world, and we can take nothing out of it. But if we have food and clothing, we will be content with that. Those who want to get rich fall into temptation and a trap and into many foolish and harmful desires that plunge people into ruin and destruction. For the love of money is a root of all kinds of evil. Some people, eager for money, have wandered from the faith and pierced themselves with many griefs.

"But you, man of God, flee from all this, and pursue righteousness, godliness, faith, love, endurance and gentleness. Fight the good fight of the faith. Take hold of the eternal life to which you were called when you made your good confession in the presence of many witnesses. In the sight of God, who gives life to everything, and of Christ Jesus, who while testifying before Pontius Pilate made the good confession, I charge you to keep this command without spot or blame until the appearing of our Lord Jesus Christ, which God will bring about in his own time—God, the blessed and only Ruler, the King of kings and Lord of lords, who alone is immortal and who lives in unapproachable light, whom no one has seen or can see. To Him be honor and might forever. Amen."
(1 Timothy 6:6-16, NIV)

"Put to death therefore what is earthly in you: sexual immorality, impurity, passion, evil desire, and covetousness, which is idolatry."
(Colossians 3:5, ESV)

"No one can serve two masters. Either he will hate the one and love the other, or he will be devoted to the one and despise the other. You cannot serve both God and money."
(Matthew 6:24, ESV)

"In the blink of an eye wealth disappears, for it will sprout wings and fly away like an eagle."
(Proverbs 23:5, NLT)

Once our flesh, pride, and greed are put in check, then we are ready to more purely surrender and follow God's calling on our lives. This foundation prepares us to steward and invest resources wisely and appropriately. When we include training and wisdom, we have powerful potential!

## Callings

I used to discount the usage of the word "calling". It seemed so . . . well, ambiguous, individual, unrefined. However, through discernment and surrender, I have come to understand how powerful and beautiful "callings" are!

Callings are catalytic movements in our hearts, minds, and souls. They are unique. They are defining. They are empowered by something greater than grit and circumstance. They are vital for us to understand.

Billy Graham had a calling. Martin Luther King, Jr., had a calling. Jeff Phillips of Iberoamerican Ministries[43] has a calling. Steph Davis, professional rock climber,[44] has a calling.

Knowing and then following our God-callings are antidotes to our pride and greed—everyone and everything goes to higher levels!

When we steward our resources in a godly manner and live generously, everyone and everything goes to higher levels!

If you do not know your calling, ask God! Then ask a friend or mentor to help you process it. If you need additional help, please contact me—your life and trajectory matters!

---

[43] www.IAmWeb.org
[44] www.StephDavis.com

## The Way of Stewardship

The way of biblical stewardship is to handle resources in the same manner as our Lord. Notice that I did not say as a financial advisor, nor as the world. Rather, in the same manner as the Lord.

The Lord's way of stewardship is to be always mindful of the Kingdom, its impact, and its progress. This may call for times of asceticism or luxuriousness, saving or spending. Yet, it is always mindful of gospel progress in our own heart and others'. It is always consistent with the heart of a loving parent.

We are the Lord's ambassadors. We are His workers. What breaks His heart should break ours. His passions should be our passions. How He treats people is how we should. How he manages resources is how we should.

How we apply this to our individual lives will vary by what is entrusted to us, the timing, and our convictions. For instance, my family has chosen a lifestyle of consuming common foods at home more than the opposite, brewing our own coffee nearly exclusively, creating and fixing things as much as we're able to on our own, etc., in order to stretch our resources, practice contentment, and to bless others. We also snow ski and own a small travel trailer. Your lifestyle may be different, and that's okay. According to randy Alcorn, "Just because they have different lifestyles, one kind of disciple is no more spiritual than the other."[45] The aim is to live and love from a pure heart, good conscience, and a sincere faith.[46]

## Love One Another

Circle of Hope is a ministry of multiplying Christian small groups in the north east area of the U.S. They take the commissioning of "one another"[47] and love through action seriously.[48] For example, church participant Caroline Butcher, a teacher and dancer, had $4,000 of credit card debt due to an injury. Circle of Hope's "Debt Annihilation Team" not only helped her pay this off, but another $96,000 of others' debt as well.[49]

---

[45] Alcorn. *Money, Possessions, and Eternity*. Tyndale, Carol Stream, page 289.
[46] 1 Timothy 1:5
[47] Hoeg. *The One Another Project*. Hoeg, Truckee.
[48] I John 3:18
[49] www.marketplace.org/2019/11/19/her-church-asked-her-to-pay-someone-elses-debt-she-was-in/

"Jesus says you can't serve both God and money, so we're choosing to serve God," said Pastor Jonny Rashid. "We want to help people get free from the bondage they have in consumer debt."

This body of believers also designates 20 percent of their collective monies to share with the "poor and lost."

The early church set the example of selling property and possessions and sharing them with all, as anyone might have a need.[50] There is wisdom, blessing, and responsibility in these actions for us today as well.

## Making It Happen

Once our hearts and objectives are pure before God, it is time to make the way of stewardship happen.

"But wait, I have so many other things to do," you might say. True, but are they as important? Are the "other" demands crucial for God? Do they have the same far-reaching results for the Kingdom as stewardship discipleship?

It is possible to make excellent progress in stewardship by simply dedicating one hour a week to these matters. You can gain this time by simply eliminating work

---

[50] Acts 2:44-45

space interruptions from your life, up to three hours a day![51] Couple this with decreasing smartphone and device interruptions, and you'll gain even more time[52] and decrease your stress.[53] Remember, stewardship is more than a ministry strategy: it involves your life too!

People commonly ask me how I do all that I do—working with many churches, with pastors, and in international ministry; writing, adventuring and more—being focused on Christ, surrendered, and available to Him and His Kingdom is first. Then, disciplines come into play, like decreasing interruptions. This is a significant part of the equation for me and something I did not fully understand until after my brain injury during my motorcycle accident in 2016.[54] The two other elements have been addressing my physical routine and embracing God's unique giftings for my life.[55,56]

---

[51] www.peoplehr.com/blog/2016/05/12/the-real-cost-of-interruptions-at-work/

[52] "Smartphone addiction, daily interruptions and self-reported Productivity." PubMed Central. 2017. www.ncbi.nlm.nih.gov/pmc/articles/PMC5800562/

[53] "How Social Media Reflects Our Daily Mood Changes." *Medical News Today*, 2017. www.medicalnewstoday.com/articles/320381.php#1

[54] https://upwardsforward.com/2017/03/31/motorcycle-crash-survived/

[55] Ephesians 4; Colossians 3:1–17

[56] *Begin: Keeping it Simple. Keeping it Real.* Jay Stearley, 2017.

My physical routine includes a healthy diet and intentional activity. My diet includes an 80/20 plant-based diet recommended by Dr. Mike Dow, author of "The Brain Fog Fix." I've become more aware and sensitive to my activity and its effects on my health. Some activities drain, and others boost. Dr. Dow wrote, "We spend so much time 'doing' that we have forgotten how important simply 'being,' or 'nondoing,' is for the brain." I have developed a habit of making a fire and sitting beside it for extended periods of time as an example of my "nondoing." There's something about a fire that feels primal—like I'm in touch with my creator, humanity, history, and myself. I also like to think of fires as the original television.

Choice of activity extends further than emotion or preference. Activities involve bodily chemicals like dopamine, serotonin, oxytocin, and endorphins.[57] Understanding how our bodies react to activities leads to greater health and ministry availability.

With the one hour a week of stewardship discipleship time, you could see ministry resources increase over 15 percent—volunteers, giving, marriage health, and more. Section III of this book provides many ideas of how

---

[57] www.huffpost.com/entry/hacking-into-your-happy-c_b_6007660

to spend these hours. Here is a stripped-down fast-track six-month outline to get going:

**Month One**

Hour 1: pray, listen, and cast vision

Hour 2: meet with an outside ministry coach and/or advisor

Hour 3: strategically plan with your team

Hour 4: strategically plan with your team and obtain the tools you need

**Month Two**

Hour 1: strategically align with your team and pray

Hour 2: meet with all staff and key leaders to communicate the stewardship vision and to call people to leadership in this area

Hour 3: send a vision-heavy, result-sharing, forward-lobbing[58] appreciation communication piece to every financial giver and ministry volunteer

Hour 4: tell a heart-moving stewardship/generosity story in large group gatherings/Sunday and provide easy next steps for people to take

## Month Three

Hour 1: review data, pray, craft, and begin sending timely messaging to each giver type/category

Hour 2: take a regular-giving person out to lunch

Hour 3: host and record a stewardship webinar for your entire congregation and the greater community

---

[58] Miller and Endicott. *Improv Leadership: How to Lead Well in Every Moment.* Zondervan, 2020.

Hour 4: meet with an outside ministry coach
and/or advisor

## Month Four

Hour 1: throw a celebration party for your team

Hour 2: utilize the right people to make pastoral
calls to every first-time giver from the
last three months

Hour 3: take a large-giving person out to lunch

Hour 4: utilize the right people to call every
lapsed giver over months one to four

## Month Five

Hour 1: host a stewardship workshop and
stream it live

Hour 2: send a thank you celebration video
to all of your financial givers

Hour 3: send a thank you celebration video
to all of your volunteers

Hour 4: pray, recraft, and ensure timely
messaging to each giver type/category

**Month Six**

Hour 1: pray, listen, and cast vision

Hour 2: provide a long-term stewardship class

Hour 3: meet with an outside ministry coach
and/or advisor

Hour 4: throw a celebration party for your team

## Conclusion

The data is in. The calling of the true God is clear . . . . be a generous steward marked by intentionality, sacrifice, and appropriate extravagance. And, for those of us residing in North America, we have an amazing opportunity and responsibility to bless far beyond beyond our organizations and personal means.[59]

The time is now—repent, model, and disciple others. Be a catalyst for others to know God, to experience His joy and devotion, and to be a blessing to many! Follow the way of the Master.

---

[59] K.P. Yohannan. *The Road to Reality*. gfa books, Carrollton, 2004.

I pray that this resource from Upwards Forward provides a boost to you and your team to attain further levels of gospel impact. A workbook that accompanies this book is available through a coaching agreement. Additional free resources are available at UpwardsForward.com, as well as information on how we partner with ministries far beyond stewardship and generosity (i.e., strategic planning, powerful communications, staffing, team building).

**Proverbs 8:1–21**

Does not wisdom call,

And understanding lift up her voice?

On top of the heights beside the way,

Where the paths meet, she takes her stand;

Beside the gates, at the opening to the city,

At the entrance of the doors, she cries out:

To you, O men, I call,

And my voice is to the sons of men.

O naive ones, understand prudence;

And, O fools, understand wisdom.

Listen, for I will speak noble things;

And the opening of my lips *will reveal* right things.

For my mouth will utter truth;

And wickedness is an abomination to my lips.

All the utterances of my mouth are in righteousness;

There is nothing crooked or perverted in them.

They are all straightforward to him who understands,

And right to those who find knowledge.

Take my instruction and not silver,

And knowledge rather than choicest gold.

For wisdom is better than jewels;

And all desirable things cannot compare with her.

I, wisdom, dwell with prudence,

And I find knowledge *and* discretion.

The fear of the Lord is to hate evil;

Pride and arrogance and the evil way

And the perverted mouth, I hate.

Counsel is mine and sound wisdom;

I am understanding, power is mine.

By me kings reign,

And rulers decree justice.

By me princes rule, and nobles,

All who judge rightly.

I love those who love me;

And those who diligently seek me will find me.

Riches and honor are with me,

Enduring wealth and righteousness.

My fruit is better than gold, even pure gold,

And my yield *better* than choicest silver.

I walk in the way of righteousness,

In the midst of the paths of justice,

To endow those who love me with wealth,

That I may fill their treasuries.

# Application Questions

## Chapter 5: Doing Business with God

1. What is your calling?

2. How do your calling and your partner organization align?

3. What do you fear about resources?

4. How does money impact your decision-making?

5. What are the top three generous things you've done for others in the last year?

6. What processes do you have in place to oversee your resources (i.e., budget, counsel)

7. What action steps should you take regarding your resources in the next month? In the next year?

# Action Items

## Chapter 5: Doing Business with God

1. Fast and pray over your, and your organization's, stewardship.

2. Review and gain clarity on your calling.

3. Review and update your resourcing practices.

4. Ensure that you are honoring God with your resources.

# SECTION II

# Leadership Workbook

"Only those who will risk going too far can possibly find out how far they can go."

T.S. Elliott

# LEADERSHIP WORKBOOK

Resources fuel a ministry: people, money, materials, and assets. If there is an abundance or scarcity, CHALLENGES exist with both realities.

How resources are managed sets a course for our lives and our organizations.

Therefore, it is prudent to be educated, intentional, and discerning in regards to STEWARDSHIP—to lead a church, an organization, and ourselves, and to help others, and, furthermore, to glorify God!

The following pages are a leadership guide for conversation, planning, and action in regards to resourcing the ministry.

# TABLE OF CONTENTS

**INTRODUCTION**

Defining the Five Conversations of Resourcing

Eight Costs of the Church's Resourcing Crisis

Two Metaphors for Resourcing Ministry

**PART 1: Ministry Evaluation**

Ministry Evaluation

Four Components to Resourcing

Defining the Four Strategic Elements

**PART 2: Understanding Reality**

Assets and Liabilities

Seven Key Monetary Analytics

Eight Key Discipleship Practices

## PART 3: Designing Your Plan

Four Strategic Elements

Designing Your Plan

Prioritize

## PART 4: Intentional Stewardship

Live the Vision

# INTRODUCTION

## Defining the Five Conversations
of Resourcing

## 1. Choosing Your Path
What is your philosophy about resources?

## 2. Defining the Vision
To what has God called your church?

## 3. Identifying Resources
What are the realities of your church's resources?

## 4. Implementing a Plan

How will you get to where you need to be?

# 5. Leading for the Long Term
What rhythms of leadership will ensure healthy ministry multiplication?

# What Does God Have to Say

Proverbs 13:11

Luke 12:15

Luke 14:13–15; 28–30

Leviticus 19:13

Proverbs 27:23

Ecclesiastes 5:10

Revelation 3:17

# Eight Costs of the Church's Resourcing Challenge

## FOUR COSTS TO THE CHURCH

Failure to resource <u>ministries</u>.

Discouraged <u>leaders</u>.

Inability to fuel <u>strategy</u>.

Thwarted impacts in the <u>community</u>.


## FOUR COSTS TO THE KINGDOM

Decreased influence in the <u>world</u>.

Restrained <u>multiplication</u>.

Immature <u>believers</u>.

Curbed <u>witness</u>.

# Two Metaphors for Resourcing Ministry

## Aspens vs. Cars

An aspen tree grove in Utah, United States, is the largest living organism on the face of planet earth. Though we only see individual trees above ground, underneath, all of their roots grow together—they are technically one tree. Aspen trees are incredible and natural multipliers.

Cars are amazing machines that changed humans' ability to cover large distances quickly in most any weather. However, unlike aspen trees, they have a limited life and do not reproduce. They take an immense amount of maintenance and have a limited life.

# PART 1: FOUR COMPONENTS

## Ministry Evaluation

**Answer each question with a "yes," "no," or "I don't know."**

1. Do we have a generous culture?

2. Do we model stewardship well?

3. Are we strategic with our resources?

4. Do we always have enough people to serve?

5. Do we do an excellent job discipling people in stewardship?

6. Do our communications cast vision and move the heart?

7. Do we have clarity and a strategic plan if resources were abundant?

8. Are our leaders generous and excellent stewards?

9. Can we do more with less?

10. Do our leaders know how to talk about money and resources?

# Defining the Four Strategic Elements

## FINANCE

The management of large amounts of money.

## CAPITAL

Wealth in the form of money or other assets owned by a person or organization that is available or contributed for a particular purpose.

## HUMANS

The people God loves and raises up for His purposes.

## CULTURE

The traditions, vibe, and social practices of a people group.

## Personal Top Four Areas of Focus

1.

2.

3.

4.

## Group Top Four Areas of Focus

1.

2.

3.

4.

# PART 2

# UNDERSTANDING REALITY

## INVESTORS VS. CONSUMERS
I Chronicles 29:1–5

## GENEROSITY VS. STINGY
ACTS 2:42–47 AND 5:1–14

## PARTNERS VS. MEMBERS
Philemon 1:4–7

# Understanding Reality

## Assets

1.

2.

3.

4.

## Liabilities

1.

2.

3.

4.

# Seven Key Monetary Analytics

1.   New Investors

2.   Lapsed Investors

3.   Legacy Investors

4.   Recurrent Investors

5.   Noninvestors

6.   Growth Trends

7.   Time-Committed Resources (Pledges)

- Investors have a stake and interest in the organization.
- Worshippers worship God with their money.
- Givers just give.

What title do you give to people who "give"?

# Eight Key Discipleship Practices

1. Culture

2. Environments

3. Connection Systems

4. Discipleship Pathways

5. Tracking Processes

6. Pastoral Oversight

7. Devoted Pursuit

8. Modeling

# PART 3

# DESIGNING YOUR PLAN

## Four Strategic Elements

1. Culture

2. Tools

3. Communications

4. Team

# Designing Your Plan

Short-term:

Mid-term:

Long-term:

# Prioritize

LONG LIST      --->      TOP THREE

# PART 4

# INTENTIONAL STEWARDSHIP

Leaders <u>model</u>.

Leaders are <u>accountable</u>.

Leaders are <u>transparent</u>.

Leaders are <u>proactive</u>.

Leaders are <u>mature</u>.

Leaders <u>resource</u>.

**Leaders can't ask of others what they are not
willing to do themselves.**

# Live the Vision

Don't simply have a vision . . . live it!

1.  Know it

2.  Own it

3.  Work it

4.  Celebrate it

# SECTION III

# Appendix 1: Stewardship Exercise

1. Pray and fast with your leadership to determine where God is calling your organization.

   1. What is God's heart?

   2. Where is repentance needed?

   3. Who has God called your church to be?

   4. What needs to happen in the next one, three, six, and twelve months?

   5. For what do people and leaders need to pray?

2. Gain clarity of your present reality (i.e., staff's perception, impact reviews, resources, demographics).

   1. How is staff culture?

   2. How is the ministry culture?

   3. What are the numbers (i.e., giving trends, weekend attendance, programming attendance)

3.  Develop a strategic plan.

    1.  Conduct a StratOp or the like (i.e., develop a

        clear understanding of how to proceed

        forward)

    2.  Invite outside help

4. Remain surrendered to the LORD, work the plan,
make adjustments consistent with the calling.

    1.  Who will champion follow-through of the

        strategic plan?

    2.  What communications need to happen along

        the way?

5. Bring the good news!

    1.  Who do you need to be to demonstrate the

        gospel?

    2.  How are you sharing the gospel?

    3.  What changes need to be made, if any?

6. Pursue partners.

   1. Create communications to value and call people to growth and action

   2. Attain and analyze financial insights (i.e., new givers, lapsed givers, giving groups)

   3. Assign administrators and reporters

   3. Schedule key communications (i.e., in-person meetings, receipt messages, programming awareness)

   4. Budget appropriately

   5. What would it look like for every attendee to feel loved and cared for?

7. Make a splash in your community.

   1. What issues are faced by your city?

   2. How can you build a fantastic reputation in your city?

3. What needs to change in your budget and discipleship to make an impact in your city?

4. Are you willing to give away (designatate) all "round-up" resources to missional activities?

8. Develop a connection culture with systems.

1. Why do people stick to a church?

2. How can you make it easier for people to connect to your ministry?

3. What needs to be updated in the connection process and communications?

4. How are you giving people a taste of your DNA?

5. Is your connection process easy and noninvasive, and does it meet the desires of newcomers? In what ways?

6.  How is your follow-up and administration of your connection system?

6.  Consider unique connection points for your diverse audience.

9. Think virtual to personal.

1.  What are people's experience of your church prior to attending?

2.  How can you increase your excellence and activity online?

3.  Where do your staff and attendees need coaching?

10. Disciple your people.

1.  How are you helping people steward resources?

2.  How are you actively pursuing monetary givers?

3. What are the hardest things for you to communicate on the topic of giving, and why?

4. Provide opportunities for people to grow (i.e., legacy planning workshop, stewardship classes and resources, budgeting workshop).

11. Celebrate often!

1. When is the last time you celebrated (i.e., baptisms, restored marriage, staff faithfulness)?

2. How can you appreciate your leaders this week?

3. Do you have ministry experiences where nothing is asked or required of people?

4. Schedule time to celebrate.

# Appendix 2: Stewardship Playbook

**Personal**

1. Fast and pray

2. Engage scripture on resources and stewardship

3. Analyze your worship and lifestyle needs versus wants

4. Repent, update, and change

5. Participate in stewardship training (i.e., Money Talks Workshop, *Financial Peace University*, Rooted, meet with a biblical steward)

6. Create and/or review a budget (i.e., make it easily accessible, share access details with whoever is appropriate in case something should happen to you, budget/prepare resources to give away at a moment's notice in the name of Jesus)

7. Begin biblical stewardship: spend, invest, give (S.I.G.)

8. Create rhythms to review your resource practices (i.e., calendar, set reminders on apps)

9. Help others (i.e., run your ideas and practices by another person, help curate stewardship training)

10. Celebrate often and thrive (i.e., enjoy a favorite restaurant, invite friends over for a dinner, purchase a discretionary desire, take a trip)

**Programming**

1. Reflect on how you are helping people win at biblical stewardship and worship

2. Create a strategic plan to help people mature (i.e., obtain an outside facilitator to lead your team through a StratOp[60] or the like, make metrics/goals visible to your team)

3. Take action to model biblical stewardship (i.e., lead from a strategic budget, resource organizations and people apart from your own, challenge people to live off $1 a day besides shelter, radically alter a gathering space to reflect a ministry partner/participant reality)

4. Cultivate opportunities for biblical stewardship training and living (i.e., provide easy first-steps to giving such as Central Chrisitan Church's

---

[60] https://patersoncenter.com/stratop/. Author, Jay Stearley is a certified facilitator.

"Generosity Rockstar" program,[61] host webinars, workshops, legacy planning, giveaway tools and tips, challenge people to start giving with a small amount of even $5 a week—one coffee shop visit)

5. Create touchpoints with training participants past the equipping (i.e., send congratulations, call to encourage, schedule an anniversary date message)

6. Regularly share stories of biblical stewardship (i.e., what people's giving is accomplishing locally and globally, a testimony of a person who is "winning" at stewardship because of equipping they've applied)

7. Train, empower, and call all ministry overseers/leaders, lay people, and volunteers to biblical stewardship (i.e., hand out or send a link to a personal budget tool, regularly communicate the stewardship goals for individuals such as having a personal reserve account for taking a vacation with cash)

8. Schedule in-person stewardship touchpoints (i.e., sermons, lunch appointments)

9. Schedule giving group appropriate events (i.e., throw an appreciation party for first-time givers for each calendar year, facilitate forums for select

---

[61] https://www.centralonline.tv/detail/?v2did=127708

biblical stewards, meet with biblical stewards and the gifted)

10. Regularly review resourcing metrics (i.e., weekly new givers, weekly contributions, monthly balance sheets)

11. Celebrate often and thrive (i.e., schedule ministry overseer/leader appreciation parties quarterly, share victories every chance you get, give bonuses from surplus)

## Communications

1. Review and evaluate your communication strategy regarding stewardship (i.e., mediums, timing, personnel, environments)

2. Update your stewardship communication strategies and team (i.e., define clear action steps, calendar initiatives far in advance)

3. Create talking points, language, and style for your ministry overseers/leaders (i.e., S.I.G., the church's desire for everyone regarding resources, generosity being an outward expression of God's heart towards people, giving your best not leftovers, training opportunities)

4. Regularly communicate with ongoing givers at a 3:1 ratio of vision and ministry impact to monetary matters (i.e., call to simply say hello, answer any questions, and pray with others; send a vision- and impact-heavy quarterly ministry update)

5. Make Sundays count with intentional, clear, and easy messaging with action points (i.e., coach people how to talk about giving during announcements, use visuals to help people know how to give, make giving a celebrated part of worship, be confident and move hearts)

6. Create a plan with custom messaging for every giving group [i.e., categorize giving groups (nongivers to long-time givers to lapsed-givers), automate communications and update templates when appropriate, share practical monetary spending tips)

7. Have a quarterly ministry financial report ready to share at any time that includes ministry impact metrics and vision

8. Update communication pieces to reflect a value of stewardship (i.e., be transparent with monetary numbers, make a stewardship roadmap available, celebrate giving group progress, utilize messaging mediums that show excellence and thoughtfulness)

9. Talk about stewardship with your overseers/leaders often

10. Celebrate often and thrive

**Data**

1. Analyze if the ministry's current information systems and practices provide the information you need in a timely manner (i.e., balance sheet, expenditures, purchasing approval practices, giver analytics)

2. Attain management systems and technologies to provide giving analytics and discipleship progress (i.e., Gyve, Mortarstone, Gloo, Online Planning Center, FellowshipOne, Church Community Builder)

3. Form a team to monitor key stewardship metrics (i.e., administrators, directors, communicators, overseers)

4. Utilize data to make decisions (i.e., planning to make a new hire, increase operational and/or reserve funds,[62] forecast expenses, know where people are growing/plateauing/dying in their

---

[62] Ross, Westerfield, Jordan. *Corporate Finance, Fifth Edition.* Irwin-McGraw-Hill, Boston, 2000, page 587.

discipleship)

5. Secure sensitive information and systems (i.e., give access rights to the correct people, have untamperable locked spaces to store sensitive information, know what vendors are doing with your information)

6. Hold ministry overseers/leaders accountable to information systems usage (i.e., utilize ministry-specific reports of key metrics, make it easy for team members to relay the information)

## Culture

1. Make talking about money and resources safe and welcomed (i.e., share stories of transformation, be open and humble, have resources available for people along their stewardship journey, communicate leadership's desire for every person, such as paying for a vacation with cash, having a reserve account or a will)

2. Help people mature in biblical stewardship and worship (i.e., take away all of your office furniture for a week, place down a tarp, cover it with dirt, and then sit on it to reflect global/partner/participants realities; take time in overseer/leader gatherings to equip and exhort in stewardship; create a mascot such as "generous george" for children's ministry

that acts out and shares stories of stewardship)

3. Lavish your ministry workers and participants every chance you get (i.e., mail personal cards to the home of overseers/leaders, create and highly care for life-giving ministry environments, purchase better food, pass forward sports and entertainment tickets)

4. Model and communicate acts of generosity, random and planned (i.e., dedicate rounded-up giving amounts to give away, take up a special offering to tip the delivery person of a gathering's meal, make information about ministry partners readily available, don't charge people for food or drinks as often as possible)

5. Celebrate individuals' progress in biblical stewardship (i.e., send congratulations cards to stewardship participants who have been able to purchase a large item, send cards to people on their annual giving first-time giver anniversary, don't put someone down for choosing to bring their own lunch, set a tone where people don't feel that they need to "Keep up with the Joneses")

6. Call for people to give of their best, not of their leftovers (i.e., give away new shoes instead of old, prepare deli meat sandwiches for those in need instead of peanut butter and jelly, challenge people

past the 10 percent tithe "training wheels" of stewardship)

7. Empower ministry overseers/leaders to be generous (i.e., give them the authority to make expenditures that serve people well, provide needed tools and environments, promote time off and health)

8. Compensate workers well (i.e., salary, paid benefits, time off, opportunities, work hours and environments, transition/retirement, etc.)

9. Give money and resources away often to high-impact needs and far-reaching impacts (i.e., sending workers to unreached people groups, sharing equipment and spaces with other ministries, etc.)

10. Celebrate often and thrive

## Strategy

1. Gain clarity and a strategy, and then align resources accordingly (i.e., participate in a StratOp, have crucial conversations)

2. Financial audit (i.e., check for accuracy, review practices, craft a strategic budget that lobs forward, review expenditure practices)

3. Partner with experts (i.e., retain a coach and/or consultant, secure a finance professional for advice and reviews, educate and equip your team)

4. Lead with faith and character (i.e., trust God for results, have solid practices that lead to achievement, never cheat, never deceive, honor God)

# Appendix 3: 52 Statistics

1. 49 percent of all church giving transactions are made with a card. [(#1-15) "Charitable Giving Statistics," Jason Firch. Nonprofits Source, 2018.]

2. 8 out of 10 people who give to churches have zero credit debt.

3. 60 percent are willing to give to their church digitally.

4. Tithers make up only 10–25 percent of a normal congregation.

5. Churches that accept tithing online increase overall donations by 32 percent.

6. Only 5 percent of Americans tithe and 80 percent only give 2 percent of their income.

7. Christians are giving at 2.5 percent of income; during the Great Depression, it was 3.3 percent.

8. Only 3–5 percent of Americans who give to their local church do so through regular tithing.

9. 3 out of 4 people who don't go to church make donations to nonprofit organizations.

10. The average giving by adults who attend U.S. Protestant churches is about $17 a week.

11. 37 percent of regular church attendees and evangelicals don't give money to a church.

12. 17 percent of American families have reduced the amount that they give to their local church.

13. 7 percent of churchgoers have dropped regular giving by 20 percent or more.

14. About 10 million tithers in the United States donate $50 billion yearly to church and nonprofits.

15. 77 percent of those who tithe give 11–20 percent or more of their income, far more than the baseline of 10 percent.

16. 7 out of 10 tithers do so based on their gross and not their net income. (PushPay, 2018)

17. Tithers only make up 10–25 percent of any congregation. (Nonprofit Source, 2018)

18. Religious giving is down about 50 percent since 1990. (*New York Times*, 2016)

19. On average, Christians give 2.5 percent of their income to churches. (Nonprofit Source, 2018)

20. Of families that make $75,000+, only 1 percent donated 10 percent of their income. (Nonprofit Source, 2018)

21. People who attend 27+ church services a year give an average of $2,935 to charity. (Philanthropy Roundtable, 2013)

22. 96 percent of practicing Christians have given to a church or nonprofit. (Barna Group, 2016)

23. 32 percent of all donations go to religious organizations. (Charity Navigator, 2016)

24. 31 percent of charitable giving happens in December. (Neon, 2016)

25. 73 percent of church giving happens throughout the week. (Pushpay, 2016)

26. Baby boomers (1946–1964) make up 41.6 percent of the donor population and 30.2 percent of the United States population. (Blackbaud, 2016)

27. Generation X (1965–1980) makes up 19 percent of all donors and accounts for 26.6 percent of the population. (Blackbaud, 2016)

28. Generation Y (1981–1997) is 7.1 percent of donors and 30.4 percent of the population of the United States. (Blackbaud, 2016)

29. 60 percent of millenials donate an average of $481 to nonprofits every year. (Qgiv, 2015)

30. Only 14 percent of churchgoers want envelopes available for checks and cash. (State of the Plate, 2016)

31. Recurring givers annually donate 42 percent more than one-time givers. (Nonprofit Source, 2018)

32. Donors aged 40–59 who would likely give online went up from 20 percent from 2010 to 2015. (Dunham+Company, 2016)

33. 39 percent of smartphone owners used their phone to pay a bill in the last month. (Snowball Fundraising, 2016)

34. 44 percent of millenials prefer to use their mobile phones to make small purchases. (Snowball Fundraising, 2016)

35. Mobile giving donations increased by 205 percent in 2015. (Snowball Fundraising, 2016)

36. Nearly one-third of U.S. Americans pay the minimum on their credit card every month. (FINRA Investor Education Foundation, 2015)

37. The number of people age 60+ with student loan debt quadrupled over the last decade. (FINRA Investor Education Foundation, 2015).

38. Only 24 percent of millenials demonstrate basic financial literacy. (National Endowment for Financial Education, 2017).

39. 74 percent of U.S. Americans write no more than one check every month. (Sharefaith, 2015).

40. About 80 percent of U.S. Americans carry $50 cash or less. (The Fundraising Coach, 2015).

41. 94 percent of respondents who say they have a "great" marriage discuss their money dreams with their spouse, compared with only 45 percent of respondents who say their marriage is "okay" or "in crisis." (Ramsey Solutions, 2018)

42. 63 percent of those with $50,000 or more in debt feel anxious about talking about their personal finances. Almost half (47 percent) of respondents with consumer debt say their level of debt creates stress and anxiety. (Ramsey Solutions, 2018)

43. 40 percent of millennial donors are enrolled in a monthly giving program. (Nonprofit Source, 2018)

44. Tithers make up only 10–25 percent of a normal congregation. (Nonprofit Source, 2018)

45. Churches that accept tithing online increase overall donations by 32 percent. (Nonprofit Source, 2018)

46. 64 percent of people volunteer locally, 9 percent internationally. (Nonprofit Source, 2018)

47. 47 percent of millennials gave through an organization's website in 2016. (Nonprofit Source, 2018)

48. Two-thirds of Americans would struggle to scrounge up $1,000 in an emergency (The Associated Press-NORC Center for Public Affairs Research).

49. 77 percent of the respondents believe that offering employee engagement opportunities is an important recruitment strategy to attract millennials. ("8 Scary Financial Statistics – and How to Avoid Becoming One." *US News & Report*, Susannah Snider, Staff Writer, 2017)

50. 30 percent of annual giving occurs in December. ("8 Scary Financial Statistics – and How to Avoid Becoming One." *US News & Report*, Susannah Snider, Staff Writer, 2017)

51. 55 percent of people who engage with nonprofits on social media end up taking some sort of action. ("8 Scary Financial Statistics – and How to Avoid Becoming One." *US News & Report*, Susannah Snider, Staff Writer, 2017)

52. 46.1 percent of churches say that using social media is their most effective method of outreach. ("8 Scary Financial Statistics – and How to Avoid Becoming One." *US News & Report*, Susannah Snider, Staff Writer, 2017)

# Appendix 4: Ten Giving Reports to Utilize

1. Giving Amount Groups

2. First-Time Givers

3. Second-Time Givers

4. Fourth-Time Givers

5. New Consistent Givers

6. Recurring Givers

7. Increased Givers

8. Decreased Givers

9. Lapsed Givers

10. Transaction Detail

## Questions

1. Do you have timely access to all of these reports?

2. How are you addressing each report (i.e.,

   communications, budgeting, discipleship)?

3. How are you communicating with each type of giver/investor?

4. How do your communications differ from first through fourth time givers, then beyond?

5. Why is it important to send additional communications about your ministry beyond an annual giving letter or campaign pledge updates?

6. Are you inspired by and passionate to participate in the mission of your ministry by your communications? Why or why not?

7. Who can you ask for help?

# Appendix 5: Money Talk Workshop

The following outline is used as a two-hour workshop. It is an excellent starting point, precursor, and promotion into more robust discipleship programs.

**Three Options: Spending, Saving, Giving**

<u>Spending</u>

- Heart Issue

- Honor God by not spending more than you make, living within your means

    - Proverbs 22:7: "The rich rules over the poor, and the borrower becomes the lender's slave."

    - Proverbs 22:26–27: "Be not one of those who gives pledges, who put up security for debts. If you have nothing with which to pay, why should your bed be taken from under you."

    - Ecclesiastes 5:5: "It is better that you should not vow then you should vow and not pay."

- Honor God by planning—establish and stick to a budget

- The Bible calls us to make plans and work them out. We also have to be flexible; God can change things, and sometimes our plans aren't His. We have to start somewhere.

  - Proverbs 6:6–8 (plan for seasons)

  - Genesis 41 (7 years of abundance, 7 years of famine, Joseph plans for the famine)

- Paul's Second Missionary Journey Example

  - Paul and Silas develop a strategic plan to visit existing churches and plant new churches in Europe

  - Twice, the Holy Spirit changes the plan they developed

  - The point—they developed a strategic plan, they moved on it, they were open to the Spirit's leading—changing their plans

- When it comes to finances, we need to do the same thing. Develop a plan (getting council and seeking wisdom), stick to the plan, be open to the Spirit's leading.

- Honor God by not coveting

  - Exodus 20:17 (one of the 10 commandments)

- o Coveting is actually telling God you're not grateful for what He's given you

- o Coveting is essentially idolatry—it's a way of trying to put something else in God's place to give us satisfaction

- o When you're tempted to covet:…

  - Confess your fleshly desire to idolize something material

  - Meditate on the gospel; look at what Jesus has already done for us

  - Thank God for everything He's already given us

- o We all are confronted with temptations to covet—but don't give in, turn to Jesus

## Saving

- Scripture doesn't command saving money but suggests it's wise and commendable (Proverbs 13:22). Scripture also says if you want to give all your money away—that is good as well.

- Suggest a rainy day fund—90 days. This isn't really saving, but just good stewardship because rainy days always come.

- Honor God by aligning any savings with His mission

- Honor God by not worrying about savings

- Honor God by retiring to give not to get—the concept of retiring isn't even in the Bible

## Giving

- Worship. Investing.

- Fun. Life change. Reward.

- Tithe (10 percent) or what? First fruits, cheerfully, sacrificially, regularly

- Getting started

- Seasons

**Budget Worksheet**

Instructions:

1. Fill out the boxes

2. Add all income

3. Subtract all expenses

4. Subtract all giving

5. Subtract all saving

6. The remaining number is the budget number.

Review and then change numbers 2–5 above to make the budget work according to your convictions and biblical concepts.

Row Total

| | | | | |
|---|---|---|---|---|
| **Income** (job, investments, other) | | | | |
| **Expenses** | | | | |
| Fixed (rent, insurance, etc.) | | | | |
| Discretionary (eating out, clothes, etc.) | | | | |
| **Giving** (local church and other) | | | | |
| **Saving** (interest bearing savings account, etc.) | | | | |
| | | | | |
| **Budget Result** (lower right box) | | | | |

After creating a budget, it can also be helpful to think through and itemize four categories to understand the financial puzzle. They are:

1. Income (wages, interest income, etc.):

2. Reserves (savings, checking, corporate stocks, etc.):

3. Long-Term (401k, Cash Value Life Insurance, etc.):

4. Insurance (Disability, Life, Auto, etc.):

# Appendix 6: 131 Bible Passages on Resources

List provided by, and with permission from, Randy Alcorn of Eternal Perspective Ministries.

1. Genesis 1:28

2. Genesis 26:12–14

3. Genesis 39:2–6

4. Exodus 16:16–20

5. Exodus 20:15–17

6. Exodus 23:3–6

7. Exodus 35:5–36:7

8. Leviticus 19:9–10

9. Leviticus 25:8–30

10. Numbers 18:12–24

11. Deuteronomy 8:7–18

12. Deuteronomy 10:14

13. Deuteronomy 14:22–29

14. Deuteronomy 15:1–11

15. Deuteronomy 16:15

16. Deuteronomy 17:14–20

17. Deuteronomy 24:14–15

18. Deuteronomy 25:13–16

19. Deuteronomy 26:12–13

20. Deuteronomy 28:1–13

21. Deuteronomy 28:15–68

22. Deuteronomy 31:20

23. 2 Samuel 24:24

24. 1 Kings 3:13

25. 2 Kings 5:20–27

26. 1 Chronicles 29:1–22

27. Ezra 1:5–6

28. Ezra 8:28

29. Nehemiah 5:3–5

30. Job 1:8–22

31. Job 41:11

32. Psalm 8:6–7

33. Psalm 16:11

34. Psalm 24:1–2

35. Psalm 37:21

36. Psalm 39:4–7

37. Psalm 49:12–20

38. Psalm 50:10–12

39. Psalm 52:7

40. Psalm 62:10

41. Proverbs 3:9–10

42. Proverbs 6:1–11

43. Proverbs 10:4

44. Proverbs 11:24–28

45. Proverbs 13:11

46. Proverbs 14:23

47. Proverbs 16:8

48. Proverbs 16:26

49. Proverbs 19:17

50. Proverbs 20:21

51. Proverbs 21:5

52. Proverbs 21:13

53. Proverbs 22:6–9

54. Proverbs 23:4–5

55. Proverbs 24:30–34

56. Proverbs 28:19–20

57. Proverbs 30:8–9

58. Ecclesiastes 2:1–11

59. Ecclesiastes 5:10–15

60. Amos 5:11–12

61. Haggai 1:2–11

62. Matthew 5:40–48

63. Matthew 6:1–18

64. Matthew 6:19–34

65. Matthew 10:8

66. Matthew 13:44–46

67. Matthew 16:24–27

68. Matthew 18:23–35

69. Matthew 19:16–30

70. Matthew 20:1–16

71. Matthew 23:23

72. Matthew 25:14–30

73. Matthew 25:31–46

74. Matthew 26:6–16

75. Mark 6:8–11

76. Mark 7:9–13

77. Mark 12:13–17

78. Mark 12:41–44

79. Luke 3:7–14

80. Luke 6:20–25

81. Luke 7:36–50

82. Luke 8:1–3

83. Luke 10:30–37

84. Luke 12:16–21

85. Luke 12:32–33

86. Luke 12:42–48

87. Luke 14:12–14

88. Luke 14:27–33

89. Luke 16:1–14

90. Luke 16:19–31

91. Luke 19:8–27

92. Luke 22:35–36

93. John 2:13–17

94. Acts 2:44–47

95. Acts 4:32–37

96. Acts 5:1–11

97. Acts 8:18–22

98. Acts 10:1–4

99. Acts 16:16–19

100.  Acts 19:18–20

101.  Acts 20:35

102.  Romans 13:1–7

103.  1 Corinthians 4:1–13

104.  1 Corinthians 9:3–22

105.  1 Corinthians 13:3

106.  1 Corinthians 16:1–4

107.  2 Corinthians 8

108.  2 Corinthians 9

109.  Philippians 4:10–19

110. 1 Thessalonians 4:11–12

111. 2 Thessalonians 3:10–12

112. 1 Timothy 3:1–3, 8

113. 1 Timothy 4:1–5

114. 1 Timothy 5:3–16

115. 1 Timothy 6:9–19

116. Hebrews 10:34–39

117. Hebrews 11:6–16

118. Hebrews 11:24–40

119. Hebrews 13:2

120. James 1:9–12

121. James 1:27

122. James 2:1–9

123. James 2:14–26

124. James 4:13–17

125. James 5:1–6

126. 2 Peter 3:10–14

127. 1 John 2:16

128. Revelation 3:17–18

129. Revelation 18:4–20

130. Revelation 21:1–6

131. Revelation 21:12–27

# Appendix 7: Leader Impact Review

## Impact Review
### Culture Trumps Performance

DATE:

Organization vision:
Organization DNA:
Organization season:

Leader and position:

- How can I help you?
- Is there anything I can clarify?
- What constructive feedback/ideas do you have about any and everything?
- Do you have any questions?
- What can improve our communication?

# Appendix 8: Ten Articles to Recommend

1. "Take the First Step"

https://www.smartaboutmoney.org/Tools/10-Basic-Steps

2. "How to Save Money: 100 Great Tips to Get You Started"

https://www.thesimpledollar.com/little-steps-100-great-tips-for-saving-money-for-those-just-getting-started/

3. "These 4 Easy Steps Will Teach You How To Budget (Finally)"

 https://www.moneyunder30.com/no-more-budgets

4. "The 50/20/30 Rule for Minimalist Budgeting"

https://blog.mint.com/saving/the-minimalist-guide-to-budgeting-in-your-20s-072016/

5. "Investing 101: A Tutorial For Beginner Investors"

https://www.investopedia.com/university/beginner/

6. "60 Simple Rules of Personal Finance"

https://www.thesimpledollar.com/sixty-simple-rules-of-per

sonal-finance/

7. "10 essential steps to manage your money the right way"

https://moneystrands.com/10-steps-manage-money-right-way/

8. "At Least as Dangerous as Porn"

https://www.desiringgod.org/articles/at-least-as-dangerous-as-porn

9. "What Does the Bible Say About Retirement"

https://www.crown.org/blog/what-does-the-bible-say-about-retirement-2/

10. "Give Yourself a $3,360 Raise this Year"

https://upwardsforward.com/2019/12/26/give-yourself-a-3360-raise-this-year/

# Appendix 9: Growing Disciples Charts

**Growth Wheel**

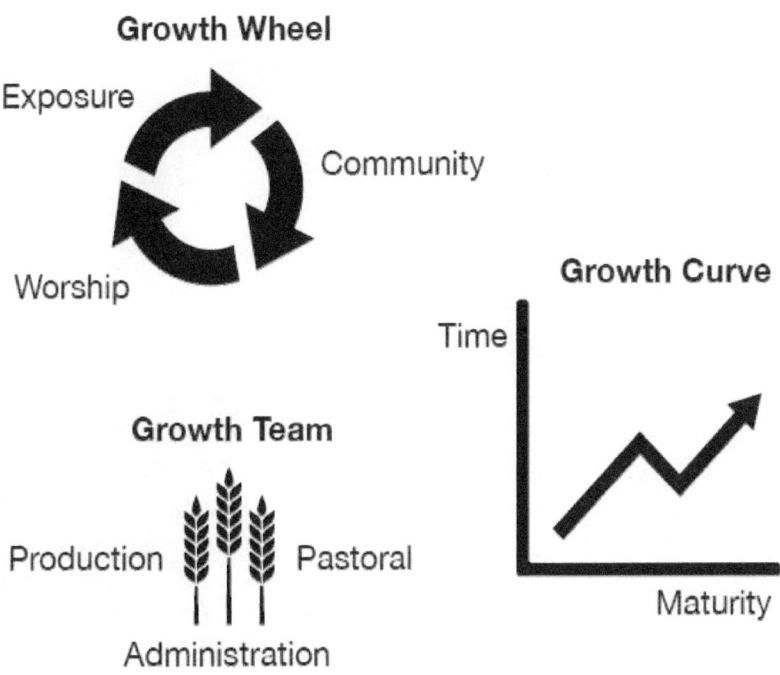

Exposure

Community

Worship

**Growth Team**

Production   Pastoral

Administration

**Growth Curve**

Time

Maturity

**Growth Sequence**

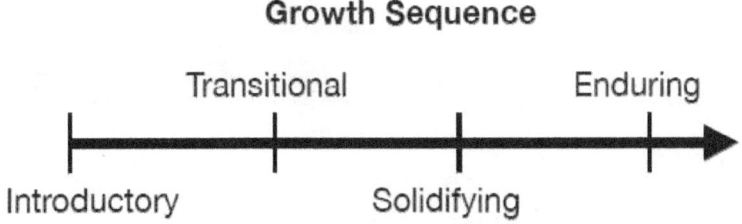

Transitional

Enduring

Introductory

Solidifying

# Appendix 10: Discipleship Roadmap

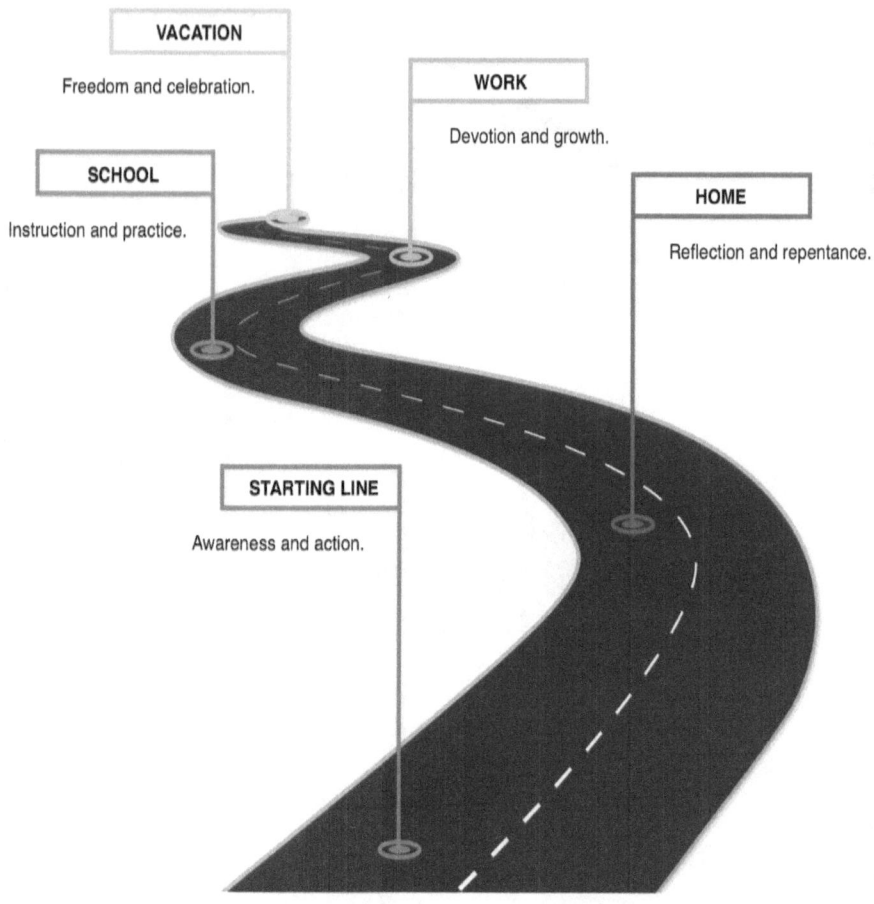

**VACATION**

Freedom and celebration.

**WORK**

Devotion and growth.

**SCHOOL**

Instruction and practice.

**HOME**

Reflection and repentance.

**STARTING LINE**

Awareness and action.

**From wherever you are to maturity.**

# Appendix 11: Deeper Discipleship Curriculum

*Deeper: An Experiential Scholarship* is a discipleship pathway to inspire further devotion to God and to equip followers of Jesus for the work of the ministry. It does so by engaging the great commandment concepts of loving the Lord with all your heart, with all of your mind, and with all of your strength (Mark 12:30).

*Deeper* consists of three areas of focus: doctrine, servant leadership, and mission. Each participant will be challenged spiritually, academically, encounter the inner-workings and leadership meetings of a Christian ministry or not-for-profit of your choosing, as well as living out Christ's call to action.

You will need a place to record your thoughts and responses to the readings and assignments. Additionally, finding someone to mentor and/or go through the material with you will enrich your experience and learnings.

The goal is to complete Deeper in six to twelve months. Self-study, organization, and drive are needed. It is recommended that you begin with *Multiply* and go through *The Exercises Volume Two: Invitations* throughout the entire experiential scholarship. Then complete the journey in whatever order suits you.

**Materials and Assignments Overview**

<u>Doctrine</u> – Core practices and knowledge of YHWH-God

● Material- Bible: Genesis, Romans, John; *Multiply*, Chan; *Bible Doctrine*, Grudem; Video, "What is Baptism," https://youtu.be/V-TLkmQpsCY.

● Assignments: Doctrine Exam on www.UpwardsForward.com/tools/; a short written response to *Multiply*, how it impacts you and how you will apply it to your life; a day of solitude and fasting; attend a gathering of another faith system.

Optional: *Water From A Deep Well*, Sittser; Apostles, Chalcedonian; and Nicene-Constantinopolitan Creeds.

<u>Servant Leadership</u> – Walking in the Spirit and helping others grow in devotion

● Material- Bible: Matthew, Ephesians, 1 & 2 Timothy, Proverbs; *The Exercises Volume Two: Invitations,* Brian Rice; *Canoeing the Mountains*, Bolsinger.

● Assignments: Love in action project (volunteer/serve/care); write one paragraph for five different leadership observations from the Bible readings; develop a one-page discipleship plan/outline for another believer; meet with two different leaders; a day of solitude and fasting; walk through the Peace Pursuit Quick Start Guide with another person where restoration and/or conflict has been with in the past (www.peacepursuit.org).

Optional: *He That Is Spiritual*, L.S. Chafer; *Celebration of Discipline*, Richard Foster; *Crucial Conversations*, Patterson, Grenny; *Money, Possessions, and Eternity*, Randy Alcorn; *Bloom*, Jay Stearley; *Sticky Teams*, Osborne.

Mission – Living with passionate purpose for Jesus and the Kingdom

● Material- Bible: Acts, 1 John, James; *Road to Reality*, K.P. Yohannan; *The Permanent Revolution*, Hirsch and Catchim; Video, "5 Issues the Church Must Stop Ignoring," https://youtu.be/tA0WK2r6mFc.

● Assignments: Love in action project (volunteer/serve/care); write about the great commission, your understanding of local and global missions, how you are and dream to engage; attend a leadership meeting of a Christian ministry or not-for-profit of
your choosing; a day of solitude and fasting; ask a person of another faith to share their beliefs with you.

Optional: *When Helping Hurts*, Corbett and Fikkert; *Don't Waste Your Life*, John Piper; *Counter Culture in a World of Unreached People Groups*, Platt.

# Appendix 12: Give Yourself a $3,360 Raise

Here are sixteen ways to improve your financial position and make a difference on earth, and ways to reap the rewards.

## Food & Drink

1. Purchase four less prepared coffees at a coffee shop = $10/mo.
2. Eat at a restaurant four fewer times = $30/mo.
3. Drink water instead of juice or soda five days a week = $10/mo.
4. Eat more plant-based foods such as rice, potatoes, and beans = $20/mo.

## Home & Transportation

1. Turn out the lights = $10/mo.
2. Run the air conditioner and/or heater less = $25/mo.
3. Decrease home services = $15/mo.
4. Make fewer trips out = $20/mo.

## Entertainment & Expendables

1. Get rid of television and web services = $50/mo.
2. Purchase your outfit at a thrift shop instead of the mall = $15/mo.
3. Go outside instead of to a movie at a theater = $10/mo.

## Extra Bonus Money Over a Year

1. Use fewer hair and skin products = $20/mo.
2. Change your own oil = $25/mo.
3. Purchase used/refurbished goods (i.e., tools, phones) = $15/mo.
4. Update a space with less (i.e., paint, decorations) = $10/mo.

## Annualized Rewards

1. Sponsor a child living without clean water, education, etc. = $40/mo.
2. Fund a reserve account for unexpected expenses or opportunities = $50/mo.
3. Pay off debts = $50/mo.
4. Take a vacation = $35/mo.
5. Give 10 percent to a nonprofit = $28/mo.
6. Save for the future = $30/mo.

7. Throw a party for your friends = $15/mo.
8. Pay for a doctor's visit or a message = $20/mo.
9. Cook a special meal each month $12/mo.

# Appendix 13: Bloom Sermon Series

**Overview:** "Bloom" is a four-part sermon series developed to 1) help people know Jesus 2) communicate God's view about resources 3) provide peace  4) motivate people to grow in worship through stewardship.

The results can be an increased stewardship quotient in peoples' lives, saved marriages, increased worship that resources the ministry, becoming talkable in your community, make it safe and normal to speak about money, and more.

Each sermon outline is just that; preachers will need to make it their own through the usage of stories and additional bible references.

## Sermon One

Title: Four Colors of Money

Main Idea: Biblical stewardship is God's way and leads to a blessed life.

Topics: Evil, Righteousness, Peace

Primary Text(s): Matthew 6:19-34; 1 Timothy 6

Teaching Points:

    1.  A Biblical Worldview on Resources
        a.  All are God's

    b.  God is in control

    c.  We are stewards

    d.  They are meant to bring life

Punchline: "The world is yours because it is Gods."

2. Four Colors of Money
   a. Black = Evil (1 Timothy 6:10)
   b. White = Righteousness (Proverbs 15:16)
   c. Blue = Worry (Matthew 6:25-27)
   d. Green = Peace (1 Timothy 6:6)

Punchline: "Green is not the only color of money."

3. The Art of Stewardship
   a. Create Your Own Reality: we make choices everyday that dictate our lives--work, spend, invest, give.
   b. Display grandeur: Everyday we have the opportunity to reflect God's greatness through our monetary actions--be wise and generous.

Punchline: "Stewardship is a practice that will make things go well for your life--marriage, health, future, friendship..."

4. Applications
   a. Believe in the good news of Jesus
   b. Become a steward of all that God extends to you

c. Know the colors of "green" and "white" in your life
d. S.I.G.
   i. Spend: needs and ability
   ii. Invest: save and multiply
   iii. Give: worship and witness

## Sermon Two

Title: Rockstar Status

Main Idea: God sees you as a "rockstar" through the good news of Jesus and He calls us to grow into spiritual maturity that includes stewardship.

Topics: Stewardship, Worship, Freedom

Primary Text(s): Ephesians 4

Teaching Points:

1. Who is a "Rockstar"
   a. Earthly: one who is successful and famous in earthly terms
   b. Heavenly: one who calls out to the Lord for salvation
   c. Identity in Christ

Punchline: Believe in the Lord Jesus and His atonement on your behalf and become far more than a "rockstar".

2. Achieving "Rockstar" Status

     a.  Earthly: motivation, creativity, skill, discipline, time, popularity

     b.  Heavenly: response, surrender, belief, devotion

Punchline: Becoming a "rockstar" doesn't happen overnight--it takes time and dedication just like stewardship.

3. A "Rockstar" Lifestyle
   a. Earthly: hedonism towards no eternal gain
   b. Heavenly: enjoying the presence and blessing of God in every breath
   c. Growing in faith and maturity
   d. The marks of a "Rockstar": joy, peace, discipline, stewardship, generosity, worship, freedom
   e. Giving, sharing, witnessing, worshipping God with our money and resources

Punchline: Walking with Jesus is better than the lifestyle of the rich and famous.

4. Applications
   a. Believe in the good news of Jesus
   b. Embrace how God sees you
   c. Live as a heavenly rockstar; walk in the ways of Jesus
   d. Worship Jesus is all that you are and have
   e. S.I.G.
      i. Spend: needs and ability

  ii. Invest: save and multiply

  iii. Give: worship and witness

## Sermon Three

Title: Being Broke is No Joke

Main Idea: To be "broke" is far more than just earthly possessions, and you have options to make it not so.

Topics: Motivations, S.I.G., Next Steps

Primary Text(s): Ecclesiastes 4:4-6, Proverbs 19:1

Teaching Points:

1. What Does it Really Mean to be "Broke"
 a. Unbelief
 b. Foolishness

 Punchline: Being truly "broke" is no joke!

2. Don't Be "Broke"
 a. Believe in the good news of Jesus
 b. Become a wise steward

 Punchline: A person who walks with Jesus and learns the art of stewardship will never be "broke."

3. Applications
 a. Believe in the good news of Jesus
 b. S.I.G.
  i. Spend: needs and ability

      ii.    Invest: save and multiply

      iii.    Give: worship and witness

  c.  Develop a budget and create rhythms to tune-it-up and review

  d.  Be free, enjoy, and crush worry

## Sermon Four

Title: Life in Bloom

Main Idea: God has created us to "be in bloom" every day

Topics: Peace, Blessing, Kingdom Impact

Primary Text(s): Genesis 15; Matthew 5:13-14, 13:1-23

Teaching Points:

1. Six Stages to Plant Growth
   a. Sprout
   b. Seeding
   c. Vegetative
   d. Budding
   e. Flowering
   f. Ripening

   Punchline: Add the nutrients to your life that you need to bloom daily.

2. Grow Money
   a. Work
   b. Budget
   c. Responsibility

d. Worship

e. Steadfastness

3. Use Money
    a. For what you need
    b. For boosting the Kingdom
    c. For worship
    d. For joy

    Punchline: Using money is a gift--enjoy!

4. Applications
    a. Stewardship is a key to freedom
    b. Bloom with life every day
    c. Grow money through wise stewardship
    d. Get help
    e. S.I.G.
        i.   Spend: needs and ability
        ii.  Invest: save and multiply
        iii. Give: worship and witness

# About the Author

Jay Stearley has over 20 years of professional experience in Christian ministry and secular sectors. He is an associate with Slingshot Group, IAM, and Symmetry Financial Group.

Jay also manages Upwards Forward, an enterprise dedicated to boosting work and people. He does this by providing strategic planning, operational support, motivational speaking, team building and development.

Prior to these callings, Jay served as an executive pastor with one of America's top 100 fastest growing churches as designated by *Outreach Magazine* (2016). He has also been a marketing director, real estate investor, NCAA Division I tennis coach, and a frontman for the rock band Aisle Seven.

Jay earned an M.B.A. in management and a B.S. in marketing from the University of Nevada, and an M.A. in Christian leadership and ministry from Western Seminary. He is wild about his wife and daughter and all activities outdoors, especially skiing, climbing, backpacking, surfing, mountain and dirt biking.

Contact Jay at www.UpwardsForward.com.

www.ingramcontent.com/pod-product-compliance
Lightning Source LLC
Chambersburg PA
CBHW021410210526
45463CB00001B/304